2016 is upon us and it's the first day; day one of our journey in a different year. For many, the journey continues, but for many it's come to an end in this realm; the physical realm. ***The journey continues upward and onward for some in the spiritual realm, but for millions even billions their journey ends literally. Death must extinguish their spirit; thus life and death begins and ends in a different realm.*** Sad yes but this is the reality of man; humans. We could not see beyond the game and games we play with our lives and the lives of others. So as January; the Month of Jan begins, death must reach home and take all who they claim as their own. Lives will be lost because there are no victors in death; the taking of your soul and spirit.

Life and death begins with us because we were given both life and death. For many life begins at birth; the birth of a child and it ends in old age with the flesh. But in truth, there is no set time for death; death can take your spirit at anytime. Therefore I've told you in another book; everywhere you go death follows, but it does not mean death have to take you.

Life and death is side by side thus your Ying and Yang on another level. And yes, it is out of the darkness that life and death came. They are not twins because one was born before the other. So there are no true twins in the truest form because you are not born at the exact same time. You may look identical, but from a time standpoint you are not true; you are different in so many ways. Time is true and it cannot be distorted or warped no matter how humans try to warp and distort it. Thus we celebrate wrong, live wrong, dream wrong, play wrong, marry wrong, die wrong, eat, breathe, sleep and drink wrong.

All that we do is wrong including the celebration of our birth and or earth strong for some and I've told you this in another book.

If you start out wrong you cannot be right in the end and I've told you this. You must end wrong if you start wrong.

No one can hide from death nor can we hide from life.

In many ways life and death are the same; without one you cannot have the other. But this is so not true because **TRUE AND GOOD LIFE DO NOT SEEK DEATH NOR DO TRUE AND GOOD LIFE WALK IN THE WAY OF DEATH. SO THEY ARE TRULY OPPOSITE IN THE TRUEST OF SENSE.**

Life is a journey and it is truly not for the weak or faint at heart. You have to be strong in life because you're not contending with physical evils alone; you have to contend with the spiritual wicked and evil as well. I know this for a fact because my journey has and have dealt me with many blows spiritually. Yes I am still standing but for how long?

So as I look to the future; my good and true tomorrow, it is my good and true will that 2016 and beyond will bring me good and happy news and good cheer, positive and good health, true happiness and care, good financial prosperity so that I can pay down my debts to death; true peace and joy; tranquility, good travels; vacations, true love always so that my truth and true love radiate and spread in a good way that it heal and touch the lives of others in a true and positive way.

It is also my hope that I will continue to have good and true life. That He Lovey will continue to breathe into me his good and true breath of life so that I will continue to give good and true; positive and uplifting in all that I do.

My good and true will for 2016 is that Lovey will shield and protect me from all wicked and evil human and breast including all wicked and evil spirit; demon. I need him to open my physical and spiritual eye fully so that I can see and know, feel and hear him right. I need him to make my dream world totally clear and true so that I do not have to decipher my dreams anymore. I need him to continue to show me my enemies and shield me from them so that I do not lay at the wayside in pain, shame and disgrace including death because of them. I need him to now help me and show me his good and true way so that I can walk to him upright in flesh and spirit clean and pure; whole the way he intended it to be. So as 2016 begins, my good and true desire is also to continue in goodness and truth with him so that I may continue to write the truth of him, educate and teach all of you clean and good, positive and whole always.

As 2016 has been ushered in for some and others await their New Year, I wish these lands the best; goodness and truth; good prosperity and wealth.

As I look to my homeland (Jamaica) in grief but yet relief; it is my hope after the destruction of this land (Jamaica) has happened, whether in 2016 or beyond that each and every Jamaican globally look into self and see their dirty ways and change their dirty clothing of self.

It is my good and true hope that they wash themselves thoroughly clean and seek forgiveness from those they have erred in the past not just for self, but for the land of Jamaica if anything is left of Jamaica.

2015 and the years before 2015 have come and gone and now it's time in year 9 (2+0+1+6 = 9) to let go of all that is spiteful and hateful. We can no longer live for hate nor can we continue to hurt our own. Life; good and true life is there for all and no one human can outlive life because life; good and true life was here long before you; humans. Truth is everlasting life and we must now live for the truth and put away all lies in order to live. We all know this so we must now do this.

Yes it grieves me to see the extent of what my own would go to to achieve fame and fortune.

Many did sell their souls by tattooing self; skin and eyes; thus accepting sin, their own death; spiritual death in the living.

<u>Many did take on the mark of the beast by tattooing that mark on their skin; flesh, thus accepting their time and death in hell in the living. By doing this; they've nullified their saving grace in life if they had one, thus voiding their contract with life and guaranteeing their place in hell with death and the demons of hell literally.</u>

Many did baptize in blood and lost their way. (Saw)

When you baptize in blood you are accepting Father, Son and Holy Ghost; the three sons of death, but in truth; the daughters of death in the spiritual realm. Because in truth; Satan has no power in the spiritual realm, she does.

Female death is deadlier than male death. When you can stop male death you cannot stop female death so easily. She is that destructive because she's the one to sink your land with all the inhabitants in it and I've told you this in some of my other books.

TRUTH IS EVERLASTING LIFE. IF YOU ARE LIVING TRUE AND CLEAN ABSOLUTELY NO ONE CAN CHARGE YOU WITH SIN. The death of J. Capri is no reason for someone to run into the whore houses of death and accept death. J. Capri was a human sacrifice unto death. She lost her life falsely so that someone would and can and will gain favour with death and the organizations of death globally. **<u>Her death was linked to money and fame. This is your Abrahamic Code and Order; THE ORDER OF DEATH.</u>**

Abraham did sacrifice is son; family for money and if you read the bible it tells you this. So the sacrificing of humans and animals will never stop. Humans will forever seek favour with death; evil for financial gain and fame.

And none of you better come tell me bout anno soh eee goh; a soh eee goh. You have to read between the lines and with comprehension. Also, every nation that deals in the bullshit of human and animal sacrifices where are they now?

Go back to Moses of your so called holy bible and see what the Babylonians did to our people of old. See what happened to them when Moses came back from the mount and saw them worshipping and or dancing around the cow; golden calf. Yes the Hindu God of Death.

Memba sey bak ome some a wi learn bout di rolling calf and or cow that come with fire.

True evil come with fiya an smoke. And yes some come without di smoke jus fiya. So I cannot comprehend why we as a nation and people cannot put one and one together. Wi noa some a di truth, but yet ignore it and wen di debil a buss wi ass now; wi a halla anna ball fi mercy. Go figure. Come on now.

In order for you to move up the ranks of the devil's organization you must kill someone of prominence. This is what you are told to do and this is what you must do.

You took a oath and you did sign a contract with death. Thus death made you and death will and can break you by any means necessary. Malcolm X ("by any means necessary").

Once you've carried out your task, death favours you. You are now protected by the organizations of death thus absolutely nothing will come of your sacrificial death. Your pledge is sealed in blood; death. So every lawyer, doctor, politician, clergy, ordinary citizen of death, nurse, banker, policeman, police chief, designer, entertainer including actors globally that is on the payroll of death you have access to.

THEREFORE, YOU'VE BECOME ONE OF THE UNTOUCHABLE!!!!

So Saw, if you are true to dancehall; then do not lie and come out of it (dancehall) due to fear and ignorance. Clean up your act and stop teaching young girls that is good to sell their vagina for money and favour. Whoredom is whoredom period. _Any woman that_

<u>promotes sex in this way is a prostitute; Delilah because you use your body for favour; financial gain, thus you sell prostitution. You have no moral values or self worth.</u>

Many of the Jamaican dancehall artists have no moral values or soul because the innocent of the innocent those you think are clean are filthy. And yes mi a drap wud fi one specific reggae artist and or female reggae artist.

<u>So because you promote immorality your listeners and or followers have become immoral just like you. And yes they will be judged just like you because they follow you. YOU ARE THE SHEEP IN WOLVES CLOTHING AND THEY ARE YOUR FOLLOWERS GOING TO THE SLAUGHTER HOUSE OF DEATH WITH YOU LITERALLY.</u>

It's truly disheartening to know that we as black people speak and teach the truth, but behind the sheep's clothing ARE WOLVES; TRUE WOLVES; DEMONS IN DESGUISE FI REAL. So I trust not my own because we profess love and unity and ARE A BUNCH OF BACKBITERS, SELL OUTS, THIEVES AND MURDERERS THAT CANNOT LIVE BY THE JAMAICAN NATIONAL ANTHEM NOR CAN WE LIVE BY AND ADHERE TO OUR OWN NATIONAL PLEDGE. Instead of helping each other; we tear down each other. We are not unified because truth; true truth lies not in any of you.

We talk the talk but yet cannot walk the walk thus we fall at the wayside and become beggars and thieves, obeah, voodoo and science workers. We accept all the filth and shit of Babylon but yet; preach and teach including sing bout CHANT WI A GOH CHANT DUNG BABYLON anna Babylon nuff a unnu a serve. UNNU PRAISE AND WORSHIP IN THE RELIGIONS OF BABYLON WITHOUT KNOWING SEY UNNU DONE HELLBOUND AREDY.

No religious leader on the face of the globe can make another human being clean; absolutely none. And none can say you are forgiven of your sins when you read in sin, pray in sin, bow down in sin, live in sin, marry and procreate in sin and die in sin. Absolutely none can help you BECAUSE A DIRTY MAN CANNOT MAKE YOU CLEAN OR HOLY IF HE OR SHE IS UNCLEAN. ABSOLUTELY NO PASTOR AND OR CLERGY IS CLEAN; THEY ARE OF THE DUNG OF THE EARTH. THUS LOVEY AND OR GOD KNOW THEM NOT. They are unclean beasts thus they teach you all that is unclean; dirty and say it is of God when they know what they teach is of death and given by death.

Strayed, but many still continue to accept blood without knowing that blood is death and water is life. You are to accept water and the waters of life because water is what cleans the flesh and your insides including your spirit.

Without water; nothing lives, not even your spirit.

Many made sacrifices unto death thus their rise to fame and popularity; their so called success.

Yes some sit in jail but what jail? Soon they will be out wreaking havoc again.

Whereas, some sit in jail because of the science and or voodoo and or obeah and the set up of others. Thus Buju Banton (Mark Myrie) must be vindicated Lovey because she wants vindication from him. And like I've said in 2015, if the homosexual community was the cause of this man being crossed with swords and if they were the cause of him going to jail unjustly; then truly make homosexuality forbidden for all. You cannot cry foul but yet willingly hurt someone that sings against your practice.

HOMOSEXUALITY IS PREACHED AND TAUGHT BY THE CLERGY OF THE GLOBE AS BEING FORBIDDEN, BUT YET NONE IN THE HOMOSEXUAL AND LESBIAN COMMUNITY GO UP AGAINST THE CHURCH AND DENOUNCE THEM. SO AS THEY HAVE DENOUNCED ONE

MAN FOR HIS ACTIONS, SO MUST THE HOMOSEXUAL COMMUNITY BE DENOUNCED.

<u>Lovey did not denounce you, but you let false profits, woops prophets and or teachers called the clergy tell you, you are not wanted and your actions are a sin.</u>

Worshipping and praising idols are a sin.

Accepting the religions of Babylon is a definite sin because they (these religions) take you to hell. Thus HELL IS FULL OF BLACK PEOPLE AND RECRUITING MORE.

And please don't say it, because some whites are black and some blacks are white. Take your pick because you have a choice which side you're on. Thus billions have not life literally. Always choose good and true life and not death. And this is not based on skin tone; hue, it's based on truth; the truth of life.

Thus, **<u>"TRUTH IS EVERLASTING LIFE"</u>** AND YOU ALL KNOW THIS.

Do not cry out for justice and be unfair in your dealings of others. Boycott his music by not buying his music and do not go to his shows, but do not send him to jail for his words. Yes words hurt, **BUT YOU LIVE THE LIFE YOU'RE TAUGHT. IF YOU ARE TAUGHT LIES AND HURT, YOU WILL GROW UP TO TELL LIES AND HURT OTHERS.**

IF YOU ARE TAUGHT TO HATE; YOU WILL GROW UP TO HATE, AND YOU WILL SEEK TO DESTROY ALL THAT YOU HATE.

So truly correct your wrong if you are involved. If you the homosexual community is truly not involved in this in anyway, then what I've written is truly null and void.

I will not extend the time, but deep down Lovey knows that repentance is given and there is penance given. Do the right thing and if penance (pay) is wanted and penance is given; then the denouncing is truly null and void.

So yes you have an out clause. I am tired of people with their bullshit telling people who they can and cannot truly love. Lovey does not stop you from truly loving; no, scrap that, he does. If you are walking on the wrong path; meaning if you have chosen the wrong person, Lovey will correct you. He will show you the person and your life with that person. And in true truth; we are not to marry anyone of Babylonian descent and heritage. Their god and gods including idols are not of the true and living god for whom I call Lovey; My Beloved, My Bunnunoonus, My Jackfruit, MY TRUE AND CLEAN JAMAICA and so much more.

Their god and gods including idols are death, and they do bring death. Thus religion, and it matters not the denomination is death. You have to accept blood. Thus religion and the religious leaders globally sell you and give you death all around. No one and or not one of them can give you water; Life, because it is truly not in them to give. Thus every facet of religion seeks to destroy and kill. They take away from the good and true life of Lovey as well as your good and true life.

None tell you the truth, nor do they seek the truth; thus they preach death and tell you, if you do not accept a dead man you cannot be saved. We believe them instead of knowing that, death is not life; it's death. Death takes life and cannot save life come on now.

Like I said, religion takes away from your life; thus they (the clergy) tell you to bow down and worship a dead man.

They tell you to eat his flesh and drink his blood (communion) thus making you a cannibal and or a vampire and a zombie; the walking dead.

Thus you were told in Revelations of your so called holy book; your bible, that Jesus was the first begotten of the dead. So because Jesus was the first begotten of the dead; he's the son of death, he has no life; he's dead, and all who follow him is dead and have no life also.

So yes every Christian of every denomination follow death because they are death; of death, the dead. They cannot have life thus water; the truth and cleanliness of life truly do not run through their veins. They accept lies; death, so they must live by death; the lies they are told by men; the gods they follow.

I truly cannot tell you people but this is truly the storm before the calm. I am truly not seeing much prophetic dreams lately. No I can't say that, I see things but I can only vaguely remember them. I can't remember this dream fully, but I am sure I dreamt something is going to happen in Canada. The dream had to do with Islamist rising up in Canada and starting a war and or something to do with the bullshit that they do globally. In the dream it seemed like it had to do with the refugees Canada is welcoming in the land. Thus I truly need to get the hell out of this country. I truly do not want to be caught up in this mess.

No country that says they are peaceful can go into another man's land that knows not peace and take their people out and say they are refugees. It's like a ticking time bomb waiting to happen. These people that are not truly peaceful, but warmongers that care not for the lives of others and the citizens of the land they live in. This goes for Christian lands as well. Thus the bullshit and shit of religion have to stop globally. <u>I refuse to buy into the Islamic and Christian God bullshit and shit. Nor will I buy into the god and gods given to humanity by desperate perverts whether male or female including religious extortionists that sell religion and god for a profit woops prophet.</u> Bleep them all because at the end of the day, my *life is truly important and absolutely none of them can save me. All they do is make me dirty and hell bound like them; thus I follow none and will follow none. I refuse to be one of their lambs going to the slaughter house of death. They want to die, let them die but I refuse to die with them. True life isn't about death; it's about good, true and clean life.*

IF YOU CANNOT KEEP TRUE PEACE IN YOUR LAND; YOU CANNOT KEEP PEACE AND TRUE PEACE IN MY LAND OR A NEXT MAN'S LAND. SO NO, REFUGEES KEEP THEM BECAUSE NO ON IS A REFUGEE PERIOD.

No one can claim refugee status in any land.

Your politicians and radicals; people cannot keep peace in your land; so why should I dirty myself by getting involved in your religious and warmonger bullshit wars?

You the people voted these bastards of crime to oversee you, so you are to blame for the conflict and conflicts in your land.

NO DIRTY PERSON CAN KEEP PEACE IN YOUR LAND OR ANY LAND FOR THAT MATTER BECAUSE THEY KNOW NOT CLEANLINESS; NOR DO THEY VALUE LIFE.

THEY HAVE NO GOOD MORALS THUS THEY CANNOT GOVERN YOU GOOD AND TRUE.

What you vote in and give rise to in the form of evil is what you get.

You get destruction and death and that is why many lands lay in ruin whilst leaving you the people; dying and in want of need of food, shelter, a proper home, medical care, proper hospital facilities and schooling and so much more.

Evil begets evil and evil spread; so don't come to me with your refugee bullshit because your underlining agenda is not true peace or peace; it is WAR.

Some of you need to watch the move I COME IN PEACE with Dolph Lundgren and see if it was peace that was truly on the alien's mind.

Many of you say you come in peace but war is your focus and agenda. You infiltrate other people's society with your religious bullshit and if we speak against your murderous profits; woops prophets; we are gunned down in cold blood. So no, I want absolutely none of you in my land and lands. And I will echo it loud and clear; this the beginning month of the New Year, 2016.

I WANT AND NEED NO BABYLONIAN WHETHER WHITE, BLACK, ASIAN OR INDIAN IN MY DOMAIN.

YOU ARE NOT WANTED, NOR ARE YOU NEEDED; SO STAY THE HELL AWAY FROM ME. AND IF I AM THE SAVING GRACE OF HUMANITY, I WILL NOT UNDER ANY CIRCUMSTANCES SAVE ANY OF YOU.

You are warmongers, liars and thieves and no one can live in peace with the lots of you. You give death; thus you are the children of death. You say you are Muslim and Muslims are peaceful but you give Muslims a bad name. <u>You are truly not true Muslims, nor are you peaceful. You give life a bad name; thus Allah, (THE BREATH OF LIFE) truly knows you not</u>.

YOU STEAL LIFE FROM THE BREATH OF LIFE THEN HAVE THE GAUL TO SAY ALLAH BE PRAISED.

Bleep the lots of you because humanity knows the lots of you praise death and take life from the Breath of Life. You mock life; thus what a day when the tables are turned and death turns on your lying and murderous asses. Therefore, it's a pity that the Breath of Life is like that; not like humans, because if it was mi an di lots of yu murder an sey Allah be praised; unnu jus drop dung soh lacka ded dawg an jus a flatta a guwey soh. No, I won't kill any of you because I am truly not death, unnu jus drop dung in epileptic fits. Thus it should be truly forbidden without prejudice that the lots of you are forbidden to say Allah which is the shortened version of Allelujah. So Lovey, if I can do this, forbid every Babylonian globally that say they are Muslim and of the Islamic faith whether Christian, Orthodox, Jew or what have you from saying Allah and Allelujah let it be done in good will without prejudice. An if dem try fi sey Allah or Allelujah mek di word and thought and written words be also forbidden fi dem fi use in any form or fashion. I petition you to make this law indefinite without end from this day, January 04, 2016 onwards infinitely and indefinitely without end. Take Allah and Allelujah (the Breath of Life) from them. Do not represent any of them come on now. This is my good and true will for 2016 and beyond. Why keep life with people that truly take life from you. Let them live as the dead because they are dead. They are void of life and truth. Dem puppa a liad an tief an dem pickney a liad an tief. So truly what say you Lovey come on now?

How can you say Allah, but yet take away from Allah?

How can you say you are of peace but yet kill?

Lovey they're all deaths people that my strupid ancestors had mercy on and let into their domain. They heard their dead cries and pleas and foolishly went against you Lovey; now look at the cost; the price we had to pay until now. Now death has spread upon land and is consuming and destroying this earth and universe.

Look at life here on earth Lovey and tell me if all of this was warranted?

We live as the dead; the sinful and deviled. We've forgotten the truth Lovey because no one told us the Babylonians were from the carcass of the dead, and no matter how you Lovey has tried with the lots of them by giving them a true home here on earth; they still take life from you and give it unto death, their father.

So yes it's time for the true Jews to leave the domain of death because in truth there is truly no life here anymore. I see the fire and or Lava rising but I cannot fully remember the dream. Now I am seeing my spirit back in the her church that is now empty. So death has not left me because like I said, I was in her church in the spirit and I could not believe I failed Lovey like that. So yes my spirit is being controlled spiritually and I have to ask Lovey why?

Why would he permit this shit to happen to me on the third day of January in the year 9, 2016?

So no, death is truly not done with me even though I am done with death. I know this is the calm before the storm because all hell is going to be unleashed on earth real soon. I know massive death is coming because I felt it in 2015 so as I let death be, I know billions of life will truly not be the same literally. *You cannot pray to death and bow down to death and not expect death. You must get death because this is the way death is. You cannot play with death either because death truly do no play.*

All that you've given to death in gist, gimmicks, publicity stunts, act and so forth, know that death keeps. Death do not let go because you praise and worship death in your acts and songs. Like I said, all that is given to death, death keeps because it is death that you praise and sing about; to. You are death's prostitute and whore thus you do all for death in hope that death will favour you and repay you in money and fame.

<u>You also lead people on the pathway of death. All who follow you; truly do not know that they are hell bound and their names are written in the book of death, thus making them and or you the child and children of death.</u>

<u>You idolize these people without knowing; you were your idols sacrifice.</u> So yes, the blind was leading the blind and the both of you must now go down to hell and burn for a time until your spirit is infinitely and indefinitely expired forevermore, never to ever rise again. You forgot that once you accept a dirty artists and follow them, their sins and dirty deeds fall upon you too. So if you had a saving grace, you no longer have a saving grace because this dirty person is whom you follow; thus making your life and home including spirit dirty also. This cannot change because this is how I know it and this is how I am relating it back to you. Thus I tell you, choose good and clean life always.

Choose good and clean; honest and true people to govern you so that you can live come on now.

IF YOU KNOW TRUTH IS EVERLASTING LIFE, WHY ARE YOU CHOOSING DIRTY OVER CLEAN?

You know a dirty person cannot make your land and home clean, so why let them govern you and take all that is good and clean from you?

A dirty person have not your best interest at heart thus nothing that they do is clean. A dirty person considers his dirty friends and family and promote them. They rob you the citizens whilst their friends and family rob the land and you of your riches and life.

Look at how some of you are living.
Look at the heartache and pain in your life.

Look at the condition of your home and country.

Look at the corruption level and the national debt load of your country.

Many lands take your money; the money of the country and fund wars, war machines, diseases, herbicides' and pesticides. Pesticides that slowly kills you and the environment you live in. So no, don't tell me about life and truth because **<u>YOU'RE ALL SLAVES; CONTROLLED SLAVES THAT CANNOT BREAK AWAY FROM THE EVIL AND CORRUPT SYSTEMS OF MEN.</u>** *You say you want good and true for self but yet; truth is not in any of you.*

Now to get on my own people due to hue and excluding Babylonians. We the black race excluding all Babylonians are a bleeping disgrace.

YOU'RE ALL CONDITIONED AND CONTROLLED SLAVES THAT CANNOT BREAK AWAY FROM YOUR SLAVE MASTERS.

You've become so corrupt and disgraceful that **<u>NOT ONE OF YOU HAVE THE FOUNDATION OF LIFE ANYMORE.</u>** We talk about slavery but in truth; **<u>YOU STILL LIVE AS SLAVES AND ACT LIKE SLAVES. YOU'RE ALL SLAVE DRIVEN BECAUSE NO TRUTH IS IN ANY OF YOU.</u>**

You've given up truth for lies; thus the majority of you have and has become bitches, whores and prostitutes for the system and cultures that made you.

And don't you dare tell me about how you are educated. **YOU'RE JUST AN EDUCATED SLAVE THAT WAS BRED TO KEEP THE REST OF THE SLAVES IN CHECK.** You just graduated from being a field slave to a house slave. You keep the lies of Massa going therefore, you still serve Massa (get it MASS); death. So you intern teach your own the death that Massa gave you to teach them. Not one of you have any respect for black culture; thus the black race truly have no set language and no true heritage to call our own. **_You're all inbred because Massa did breed a lot of you; your ancestors for his own personal gain and welfare. You were his profit margin in hell and here on earth and you still are. Consequently, none in the black race know this until this day._**

The lots of you run around Massa and kiss his ass because we truly do not have our own black enterprise that we can stand behind and call our own. **AND EVEN IF WE TRY WE ARE BROKEN DOWN; SET UP TO FAIL BECAUSE THE BLACK MAN AND THE**

BLACK WOMAN MUST NOT HAVE ANYTHING PROSPEROUS FOR SELF; THEIR OWN.

And don't you dare tell me to look at Black America because Black America owns shit. All you see are just puppets put in the forefront for you the faint at heart to have a little hope. WHEN THE SYSTEM IS DONE USING THEM, THEY ARE SPAT OUT LIKE DEAD MEAT AND OR THE CARCASS OF THE DEAD. Look at many of your black actors and producers of today and yesteryear.

Look at many of your musicians and or singers of yesteryear and today. How many have died due to drugs and alcohol.

Many are still strung out on drugs and alcohol and if they are not, they have to swing and sway both ways on the fence.

Like Bob Marley said, "WHAT WE KNOW IS WHAT THEY TELL US."

So in essence; we as a race and people don't know shit. And many of the books that you read is shit because they don't tell you the truth of you as a people and nation.

You don't truly know **BECAUSE IF YOU DON'T SELL OUT AND COME THEIR WAY, THEY DESTROY YOUR REPUTATION AND CHARACTER.** Man do they ever pay people to assonate your character and all that you've built. So in all that you do, they do all to take you down including use your own against you. They do everything to break you. **_Yes this is sad but it's the reality of our own black people._** **WE BUILT SOCIETIES OF MEN INSTEAD OF BUILDING SOCIETIES OF SELF; BLACK SOCIETIES THAT IS BASED ON GOOD MORAL VALUES AND MORALITY.**

Instead of leaving their evil societies that has no morals behind; we bask in them, and when we are beat up and killed we wonder why.

Instead of respecting what we have including self, we sell our self short and degrade the legacy that some of our forefathers built for us.

Instead of respecting our black men and women; we disrespect them, slander them without knowing that behind closed doors they're saying; "it's just another nigger and buffoon that we can play; do our own bidding." They pretend to like you, but deep down they truly hate you. <u>*You are their profit margin and could never be their equal.*</u>

Some are just a good time in bed because at the end of the day, he's got the prenup that states your self worth to him her. So the clowning and games truly never stop.

Instead of setting good moral values for self; we teach our children to accept their gods, their heritage, their culture, hair and everything, whilst giving up our good up good up own.

Yes I can go on, but I won't go on because this is truly not the day for it in my book. Don't need to be long winded in 2016. And I truly don't think I'll be writing much in 2016. Truly don't need to.

So nothing's new under the sun when it comes to my black own. What the devil and his people wants they get because the devil made sure he got your resources and vote; thus he has the financial resources to buy the lots of you literally. So no matter how we as a people look at it, we are traded; bought and sold.

We are a commodity; thus the global stock markets of the elites and super elites. And yes thus is truly a shame.

As blacks we have no unity because we're mixed up and confused; told lies of us being from this tribe and that tribe. Look at how lowly the black race have become. Thus the African lies has to stop.

Now let me ask all of you in the black race whether Black, White or Chinese this, how can the creators of this universe including earth become the dung of humanity; this earth?

If we the black race was so lowly and stupid, why is it that every race on the face of this planet including our own is eliminating us?

Why are we so hated?
What make the next race better than you and me?

What makes their hair, skin, culture, language, way of praise and worship, heritage, god and gods bet than ours; what He Lovey has given us for our own?

We have our land, dem want eee.

Wi ha wi hair dem want eee.

Wi ha wi music dem want eee an now dem inna it; dem pollute it.

Wi ha wi language dem want eee.

Wi ha wi good up good up skin dem want eee. Den tell wi sey wi skin nuh pretty and wi soh fool fool wi believe dem. Everything wi ha dem want, but yet hate wi soh.

Wi ha wi nappy hair that is a natural electric current that stands upward to Lovey at nights and dem tell wi sey wi hair noh good. Our hair is our natural communication outlet to Lovey, what makes it so bad?

Our vibration is not the same as the next man's because they truly do not have black vibe. Our vibration is our vibrations, thus our music is different, our culture is truly different, our way of dress, speech, hygiene, cooking, mating, singing, dancing is truly different. All this we know but yet overlook and I truly do not know why.

So, if we are so bad and hated, leave us the bleep alone. Don't dress like us, don't comb your hair like us, don't date our men and women, don't eat our food, don't vacation in our lands, don't want or need anything of ours including our ganja come on now.

You hate us but want to be included in our realm; all that we do. That doesn't make any sense. SO TRULY DON'T HATE US BECAUSE WE ARE TRULY GORGEOUS AND YOU'RE TRULY UGLY COME ON NOW. Hate is ugly and anyone that hates based on hue or anything for that matter is ugly. No, I shouldn't say that because Sins I loathe, despise and hate so that would make me ugly.

NOT!!!!

Sins are truly ugly.

And no, this is not a racial rant in 2016. I am just showing you just how hypocritical this hatred of blacks and yes whites is and or are.

Oh man this is supposed to be my good and true will for 2016 and beyond and it has turned out to be something else. And don't you dare say ya think.

Yes it is my hope that my homeland; the people of my homeland will put down their sinful ways and look into self and do better for self.

It is my hope that they will stop selling sin and stop leading the children and people of Jamaica astray; to hell. No one deserves hell because if you think your life is hell here on earth; truly don't wait or want to go to hell. Life there is brutal and if you've read MY GOOD AND TRUE WILL AND I NEED you will know just how brutal the spiritual wicked can be. Mi batta bruise and I am barely making it much less you.

It's January 08, 2016 and family, I more than over stand what Bob Marley was taking about when he told us about spiritual wickedness. I thought I went through brutality in the latter half of December 2015, but nothing could prepare me for what I went through January 6-7. Thus I've told you in some of my other books, the closest thing to death (in the living) is sickness. I was so sick on Wednesday that my spirit wanted to cry out for death, but all I could do was cry out to Lovey and ask him why he's forsaken me. I could not cry out to death though my spirit wanted me to. **<u>Spiritual wickedness is nothing we should have to go through because you are left broken.</u>** This isn't a test; this is hatred. Therefore, no one can come to me and tell me that God don't give you more than you can bare. God gives you way more than you can bare. He does allow the forces of hell to rain down terror on you in the living.

So for you people that keep telling others that God don't give you more than you can bare; truly stop this nonsense. Not one of you have gone through hell like I have and still going through it.

Not one of you has gone through hell like some people. Some of these people are still going through hell. There is a spiritual hell and a physical hell and when both are unleashed on you here on earth; no prayer can save you. You have to go through it. Some people don't make it out alive. This hell no preacher man or woman can tell you about because they've never been there. When the forces of evil lock you in you have to wait until your time is up before you are released. Not even God can save you because he does permit this to happen to you.

He Lovey, God cannot tell me this is a test because like I said, no human being should have to go through this to prove their worth to him. So no matter which way you look at it; both good and evil go through hell. The only difference with this is, if that good person makes it, he or she is guaranteed a place with Lovey and that everlasting and or eternal life.

The children of death do not make it; thus they are hell bound indefinitely. Once you've chosen hell and if there is no redemption of sin, then you cannot be redeemed in the living and in death. You have absolutely no saving grace because none is given.

Yes I did see the hell. I kept dreaming about the evil that surrounded me, but never in my wildest dream was I expecting what I got. I've cried more in this month than I've cried in all of 2015 I think and the year has just begun.

When you are all alone and you have to go through this, no. No one should have to go through this on earth. I had to ask God; Lovey, what wrong did I do that was so vile and wicked for me to go through this.

People, when your bible talked about what Job went through, don't take it lightly. Truly don't. You truly don't know and you truly don't want to go through this. Evil do everything for you to fail because they leave you broken and some do die. If you think you have trials and tribulations now, truly don't want to face spiritual tribulations. **_I beg of you, don't._** I have no one to support me or lean on. All I can do is cry and tell Lovey, no more, I cannot face anymore. I can't go through it.

It's like a dead weight is on you. I don't know if you've heard the story of Atlas holding up the world; earth. The dead weight is like that.

I truly don't know why I have to face this. And it seems like it will not stop. It's like you are trying but everything just come down on you all at once. You're left ruined and you can't figure it out.

You're left without hope and a broken trail; pathway. It's like God; Lovey has abandoned you too. He's there with you in the physical storms but when it comes to your spiritual battles; tribulations, he's truly not there. You are left alone to go through this battle alone. You're bruised sanity wise, you're broken health and financial wise, you're broken spiritual wise; all that's left is for you go give up, but you can't; you have to endure. But for how long before you keel over and die?

Thus why Lovey, why leave us broken and destitute if we are trying to reach you?

Why do you not listen?

Truly listen to Tamela Mann's song TAKE ME TO KING. Listen man come on now. When we are left broken and tried, what do we have left?

We are battered and bruised and it's time for this bullshit to stop. You can't want us to come to you then turn around and beat us up; whip us like slaves and say this is what you get for disobedience and we should be grateful that you take us back. You don't like suffering and pain so why should we? I've told you time and time again, if you do not teach properly, how are we to learn and know the truth?

If all we are given are lies, we will grow up to tell lies and continue teaching others in those lies. You know this but you have not done a good job in changing this come on now.

You cannot say you want us to live clean and not give us cleanliness to live by in the first place.

IN ORDER FOR US TO LIVE CLEAN WE HAVE TO START OUT CLEAN.

Yes we are to blame as humans for many things, but you too as God, Good God and Allelujah; Lovey has to take some of the blame too. You too did wrong. You have to be fair and just all around. I've pride myself in being open and honest with you. So have others and you are the one to let us down. You are the one to let us get beat up on by physical and spiritual wickedness, and when we fall and or fail you, you get angry.

IF WE DO NOT HAVE THE RIGHT AND PROPER TOOLS TO LIVE, HOW CAN WE LIVE RIGHT?

IF YOU ARE NOT TALKING, HOW THE HELL ARE WE TO KNOW?

I cannot combat spiritual evil and you know this. Instead of helping me, you let the spiritual wicked find me each and every year. You allow them to unleash every arsenal in their weapons on me. So now tell me, how am I to feel and think as a human and as your child; daughter?

Yes I am seeing different things but more evil than good. Dreamt about Taurus Riley and his tattoos. I told him I wrote about him in some of my books. In the dream he had these black tattoos on his skin that is different from the ones he has in real life. I truly don't want to get too much into my dreams because they are long. All in all, in this dream, we were walking and talking. I ended up walking bare feet because he took my brown sandals and it began to rain and I got wet. I did not have an umbrella. When I did find them (my sandals), they were not the right ones, they were two different feet and I could not wear them. Upon taking off the wrong sandals he (Tarrus) brought me my right pair and we continued to walk together. That was when I saw his different tattoos and I told him, I wrote about him in some of my books. I told him I don't understand why a man that sings conscious music would tattoos himself. He never gave me an answer and it was then that I thought I saw Damian Marley. I was excited to see him. I believe he was with this girl and I went to go hug Damian but

Tarrus pushed me out of the way so that I did not get to hug him. See I wanted to tell him (Damian Marley) my take on the boat cruise that they did. I wanted him to know it was an excellent idea and it worked. Suffice it to say, the push Tarrus pushed me out the way, it was another person, another dreadlocks and I did not hug him, but we pounded fist if that's the right way to say it.

We touched fist.

Dreamt Taraji P. Henson and that she was caught up in drugs and was in court. In the end you could see blood oozing from her eyes with puss and she did not want anyone to see it or know. The way she was walking was pretty horrible. So who knows what's going on with her.

Dreamt Diddy or P Diddy or whatever name he is using. I was with this white gentleman in this nice place. P Diddy came up. In the dream he spent 5 years in Africa. So because of the years spent in Africa, I was telling the white gentleman I was with that I bet he's going to start making African Clothing. Oh yeah, in the dream, P. Diddy was dressed in black.

My dreams are music centred and I so have to be careful because one involved theft of a highly and well known powerful producer or top Jamaican honcho. His friends; good friends that he trusted went into his safe and took all his money. They did not take his vintage cars or jewelry only his money. In the dream I saw the guys and knew they were going to take the money because I was an accomplice. The money they hid in three different places and did not put it in the bank like I told them to. This man trusted these guys that he did not suspect they took the money until it was too late. Yes he caught me but I got off and left. There is more to the dream but suffice it to say; no one got caught. I know this is a dream in a dream and I truly have to be careful in my travels that I do solo.

Dreamt I was with this white guy that was dressed in black. It's like I knew him and he reminded me of my school mate; tall and strong. We were at Niagara Falls and the Falls had dried up. There was no Maid of the Mist and you could walk on the rocks. It seemed like winter time but it wasn't truly winter because we weren't dressed in winter clothing. In the dream it's as if people left their canoe like boats on the water and it looked so disgusting; the boats because they were decaying. And like I said there was no water. Whatever water that was there it was gross, greenish muddy and yucky. So we had to walk up these steps to leave the area where the water was once flowing and abundant.

Truly don't know what this dream means and I am so not going to decipher any. Just going to watch and see.

So to my people of my homeland and to the global citizens of the world; truly look into yourself and do all to preserve your life. Please stop following evil if you can. Evil is bringing you to the slaughter house of death and that is what's happening right now. Yes you've been hurt but stop letting your political leaders, family, friends, musical and theatrical artists lead you astray.

YOUR LIFE IS WORTH IT SO SECURE IT HERE ON EARTH.

Yes the battle is fierce but it is going to get harsher; the forces of hell must be unleashed on earth. Right now it's the calm before the storm and many of you will not make it. Instead of preserving life many of you gave it up foolishly. Stop preserving death and preserve you.

The New World Order of Death must begin because we as humans allowed our future to be eroded beyond repair. We gave our lives over to death and death must take us. We cannot remain on earth because there is no future to be had for billions of you. There is no future to be had for your future generations either. So as life ends for you; life ends for them also. This is the truth and this truth you must know before you go forever ever without end. Our legacy here on earth is death because we gave death's people control over our lives.

There is no life in death and if death cannot live; neither can you, you must die with death and this is truly what's going to happen to billions of you.

As Jamaicans we did break our vow to God and Man and for this Jamaica and you the people of Jamaica must pay.

So yes as 2016 begins it is my hope that Jamaicans globally put down the gun violence, pain and hatred, obeah and science business, the jealousy, human sacrifices and animal sacrifices they deal in, the feeding of the dead that they deal in, the using of the dead that they deal in, the pedophilia they deal in, the raping and murdering of the young and elderly that they deal in, the religious condemnation of self that they deal in, the corruption that they deal in, the unnecessary babies that they have and cannot feed that they deal in, the whoredom and beheading that they deal in, the willful murders that they commit and so much more, I hope 2016 see them put these things down and heal; truly heal so that they can live. Jamaica must rise but one cannot do it; all must want and need a positive change.

We can no longer have the wicked and evil rape us of our lives come on now.

Life is worth it and if you don't have life in the living, you cannot have life in death come on now.

It's time for the good and true to have a positive change in life Lovey and we cannot have it without you. You must be on the same page with us and we must be on the same page with you. The one sided disarray must stop now come on now. We cannot say God but yet have no god; can't find you.

Wi a sey Gad and wey yu dey?
Wey yu dey come on now?

Life isn't a joke; so stop letting humans disrespect life come on now. How the hell can we say Gad and can't connect with you in the right way?

We call on you but yet our prayers are not answered. It's like our communication line with you is severed; cannot be repaired and this is truly wrong on your part. Don't want us to come to you and when we make the effort by starting to walk right and talk right, you push us off our path and or let negative influences come into our path and knock us off our way to you. If we are walking right let us continue to walk right and true; clean to you come on now.

Yes I more than comprehend the lack of answer because the God some a wi call pan anno yu. I get it, but where is our true communication line with you; the true and living God come on now?

Why leave us calling out to you in vain?

Now tell me this; if you truly wanted us to truly reach you; find you, would you not have given us the right communication line to you?

Remember he wrote the 1 876 number to you in my hand, and still I can't use that number to get to you. So why did he lie to me?

Why did he give me something; a number that I truly cannot use? Lies are sins; you and I know this Lovey.

As God, <u>YOU CANNOT GIVE US THINGS WE CANNOT USE.</u> THAT GIVING THAT WE CANNOT USE <u>IS A LIE ON YOUR PART</u> THUS MAKING YOU FALSE; UNTRUE. Hence that giving becomes a sin on your part and this Lovey you as God need to know. If you give, give truthfully and clean not false.

If you truly cared, would you not have given us the right and correct telephone number to you?

We wouldn't be hindered in reaching you. But yet we are, and you truly don't seem to care in my book.

So what say you in the care and loving so department?

Yes I am at odds with Lovey and maybe this is why hell is being unleashed on me. MY GOOD AND TRUE WILL AND I NEED should have been uploaded to Lulu.com on December 27th but was uploaded on December 26th and Lovey will not let me live this down. From the latter part of December to January he's reminded me that what's done is done and you cannot go back and change the past. Basically he's telling me that mistakes made cannot be changed once the time has elapsed. For example, I could have reuploaded the book on December 27 but I did not. Everything would have been okay if I did this but, I did not. December 28th came and it was too late. Like I said in the book previous to this, I was right with Lulu but I was not right with Lovey and he's mad.

But like I said to Lovey, we did not start off right. I started off right with her because she chose Lulu for me. When I deleted my first book off Lulu.com she made sure she showed me what things would be like. She was honest with me from the get go; Lovey was not.

<u>Lovey asked me to write him a book not once but twice. He Lovey did not tell me how to write the book. I told him, I would not lie for him nor will I tell lies for him and on him. I told him I will only write the truth.</u>

In all of my dealings with Lovey, he never said, Michelle this is what I want and need you to write word for word. I've seen and read the message on the school wall and gave that message to you word for word.

I've had to figure things out and decipher dreams. Sometimes I did decipher wrong. I had to walk alone and in all that I've done, I've had my prosperity taken from me by my own black men in the spiritual realm.

What I've done to secure Lovey in truth, my own black men rob me of it and he Lovey allows this to happen. I've battled ill health, loneliness, insanity in my book, depression in my book, disrespect from children and others.

I've had people look down on me, class me as evil from an early age and I am sure once these books get out, many of you will class me and define me as evil; the wicked and evil demon of this world. You will do all to eliminate me and hurt me. Hey been through it spiritually; so nothing surprises me or will surprise me with the set up and the using of my children against me.

Yes it's regretful that many of you cannot see the truth and know the truth. What I've faced, none of you have faced here on earth and I do not wish this on any of you.

Many of you say you are strong and can withstand anything. <u>But physical strength is nothing compared to spiritual beating and the forces of evil.</u> Spiritual beating you truly do not want to go through. Think of Job because I know what he went through and no amount of prayer, obeah, voodoo, well wishes, hugs and good thought can help you. <u>I've told you, not even God can help you through this. You must go through this beating alone because all that evil has, they're going to unleash it on you in order for you to break and come their way.</u>

Therefore, it is imperative for you to know the truth of God; Lovey because if you know not the truth, you will break; die. If you do not live for the truth and truly trust Lovey, you will not make it out alive. This is why you are told of heaven and hell. Heaven here on earth which is spiritual hell and Hell; that which is made of spiritual fire; the place your spirit go to die after it has shed the flesh. This hell there is no water to quench your thirst; thus strive not to go there.

YOUR SPIRIT NEEDS WATER IN ORDER TO LIVE, SO TRULY STRIVE NOT TO GO TO HELL AND BURN.

There is only one way in and absolutely no way out.

Death is an out you are saying.

Death is no way out. Death is death; the extinction of your life. So make sure your good outweighs your evils because if your evils outweigh your good, you have no chance in hell to be saved. Like I've said time and time again in some of my other books, if I am the saving grace for humanity; I will not save anyone that is wicked and evil. So know which side you stand and lay on come on now.

I've been through too much at the hands of wicked and evil people to save any. You paid me and others with evil; so why would I save you for you to continue on with your wicked and evil ways. Someone is doing right and good by you and for you, help that person up so that they can continue to help you and lift you up. Do not take them out of the picture.

When that goodness is gone, what do you have left?

Who's going to help you or even save you?

When you take away goodness from this life and or earth, you are taking away life from you, this earth and universe and more importantly Lovey.

When you take away and or kill a good life, you are taking away from the goodness of this earth; you.

We know evil cannot maintain life; all evil can do is destroy and kill all life including yours. So why take away good life from life; you? Add to goodness not take away from goodness come on now.

Now take a good look at earth and tell me; WHERE HAVE ALL THE GOOD PLACES GONE? LIFE IS FLEEING FROM EARTH AND NOT ONE OF YOU REALIZE THIS.

No it's not you are saying.

Don't bank on Jesus, just look at the killings and insanity worldwide. Look at the restrictions made on your life health wise, financially, emotionally and spiritually. <u>Look at what you and this earth has lost. Now look at the environment and the depleting</u>

resources of earth and tell me, what has life gained in the process?

We build and consume in greed. Sin

We live immorally and we die immorally. Sin

We live in hate and die in hate. Sin

We live religiously. Sin
Hate and kill religiously. Sin

We marry wrong and die wrong. Sin

We love wrong thus hate. Sin

We tell lies and teach others these lies. Sin
We even say these lies are traditions; thus sin, generational lies and sins that are handed down from generation to generation. Death

Many are left to turn beggars and thieves. Sin

Now all that you've worked for will be taken from you because MAN SAY MONEY IS THE ROOT OF ALL EVIL. BUT I SAY UNTO YOU, MAN; THE GREED OF MAN IS THE ROOT AND CAUSE OF ALL EVIL.

No tree was created evil, but Man was born with evil Will; the darkness of death. Thus man; humans, like to control, dominate, destroy and kill.

So yes, while many lands devalue the currency of other lands and put their currency on top; it is my good and true will for 2016 and beyond that good and true lands do not become cashless. Evil lands can stay cashless because underneath their schemes, they only seek to rob the poor of what they've worked so damned hard for; that which they've put down for the future to help them; self. Therefore, they (the rich that control the global financial institutions) must implement their New World Order of Dominance and Control; Poverty, in order to rob you the poor of society.

Every society needs cash. It's this cash and or money that you worked for. When you take a dollar from the bank, you are seeing the fruits of your honest and hard labour. Money is valued because it is truly earned by some. You can look upon it and feel good that you can pay your bills and have a cent left over for a rainy day. Yes to some the penny is not much, but one penny gets you two until you have a dollar. That dollar becomes two and three and so forth. Yes sometimes you may have to touch that dollar but by the end of the week, you have two more come on now. Thus blessings come in many forms and ways.

Yes I am down on Lovey, but I am not going to turn against him. Although he was not with me in my spiritual storms he was with me in my physical ones and I cannot be ungrateful for that.

Through my spiritual storms it's him I had to cry out to. I made him my beating stick; thus he was my spiritual shield as well even though I did not know it at the time.

So, if you are not grateful and thankful for life; then truly good luck to many of you. Nuff a wi sey wi true but deep down, the heart is filthy; unclean, so you can never be true and never true in the first place.

Goodness I live for; thus those who are truly good to me I have to secure them and ask Lovey to secure their land and people also.

I know goodness; therefore, I try to do all the good I can do. Not for reward but because goodness is all I truly know and I truly do not want to give this up no matter what. I truly do not need Lovey's blessings for the good that I do. All I need is to know is that the good I do for some; you truly help in a positive and good way so that you can flourish and help self and others come on now.

In choosing me to write, Lovey never said, Michelle, if you choose to take up this task; writing for me, you will be battered and bruised, you would be beaten spiritually, financially, health wise, emotionally, physically, mentally amongst other things. You will be left alone to find your way; the demons of hell will find you and do all to kill you so that you will fail me.

He did not tell me that the things he gave to me spiritually I would not receive physically.

He did not tell me that all would be taken from me to break me.

He did not tell me that he would not be there for me spiritually through my ordeals.

Many things he Lovey left out. So no, he did not start off true with me; thus I could not end true with him and he knows this. <u>Absolutely no one can make our wrongs right. They are recorded as wrongs and they stay as wrongs on our record. Maybe this is what he Lovey wants me to let you all know.</u>

So whatever you do, start things off right in order to end right. **<u>Wrongs cannot be right and rights cannot be wrong; it's impossible.</u>**

I know you are saying Lovey cannot be wrong and I am telling you he is wrong and this is from my perspective.

To me, in all of his creating, He Lovey should have started off creation clean; no I should not say that. Truly forgive me Lovey because evil is born, it was never created. What I am saying is, Lovey should have never given MAN evil will. He should have ensured that good and evil never meet and procreate.

In all that I see, I've yet to see the residence of God; Lovey.

The Crystal City I've seen because it's a black female that watches over this land and or city.

I've seen the brides of heaven and they are all black females clothed in white with white sandals.

I've seen the children of God; Lovey and they are all black females with the exception of one bi-racial child.

I've seen the lands and or the boundaries of lands paved in gold in Africa.

I've seen the deceit of Babylon.

I've seen Satan.

I've seen male and female death.

I've seen Zion and the inside of Zion.

I've seen the downfall of Zion; black Zion.

I've seen the scrolls and or book of life and the names written in the book of life.

I've seen the birth of life, but I've never seen the inside of Lovey's domain. Yes the trust is there, but he should have prepared me for the beatings I was going to get.

Do I regret any of this?

Just me not knowing this before I had kids, but I cannot live in regret. It's my hope that these books help you to make the right decision for you. And no, I truly do not regret the choice I made. If I did, I would not be truly true. Despite my pain and sufferings, I truly do truly love Lovey with my good and true heart and he knows this. So we are all good; good to go as we Jamaicans would say.

I've told you, I am not the final decision maker in all of this. Besides, Lovey is not as temperamental as me; nor does he act on certain things right away when it comes to my asking. Many things he does not act on at all as far as I can see. **THUS ALL IN HUMANITY HAVE HOPE.**

You can try and save yourself despite what I write. LIKE I'VE TOLD YOU TIME AND TIME AGAIN IN SOME OF MY OTHER BOOKS; **LOVEY LOCKS NO ONE OUT OF HIS KINGDOM AND ABODE, WE ARE THE ONES TO LOCK OUR SELF OUT WITH OUR SINS; LIES.**

Everyone can save them self, but is it everyone that truly wants to be saved?

Many of us see the fire and know the fire, but still go into it anyway and this is truly wrong. If you don't have to get burned, why want to and this is what Lovey is trying to show us.

His way is easy I know this; it's the evil forces around us that makes it truly hard and brutal for us to stay on the path of truth come on now.

You cannot say you love him Lovey and praise another god.

You cannot say you praise and worship him Lovey but render evil unto others.

You cannot say you know and believe in him and cheat on him Lovey and your spouse. That's not truth, that's hatred come on now.

You have the foundation and basis of life and you were given life, so <u>LET THE DICTATORS GO OUT OF YOUR LIFE.</u>

Dictators destroy and kill you.

THEY BRUTALLY ABUSE YOU.

They take away your fundamental rights and freedom from you.

They impose martial law on you and your family.

You cannot think for self; they have to do the thinking for you.

You are controlled and told what to do.

You are left without life, because there is no life under their control.

If you do not adhere to their wicked and sinful laws and rules, you are punished and killed.

You cannot speak out against your dictator because they control you, your land and the countries resources.

Truth is of no worth or value to them. Thus the truth is muzzled and lies are their mainstay and sustenance.

Under your dictator you live poor, are rationed; thus you've become valueless; their slave that has no self worth.

Your life if not yours, it's theirs because they can take your life from you at any given time and they do on a daily basis. You are censored and can only see what they show you and you can only read what they give you to read.

Freedom you cry to yourself, you want freedom, but no freedom comes. No one realize that no one can be free in a controlled environment and society.

People need to talk, exchange good ideas and values.

Lovey gave us all freedom, but we as humans allow others to take our freedom from us.

They make us live in fear and turmoil and not one can see the hurt they are causing you the citizen and the land; environment you live in.

Many of you are used as experiments like lab rats.

Many of you, you have no right in their penal systems because crazy and inhumane people called doctors experiment on you at will.

Your governments care not for you because they say, go ahead, use them; they are valueless and have no self worth or of worth to the community and or environment you live in.

Yes there is a lot more but I truly do not want to go on because <u>the societies of men are truly sickening and disgusting. We feed evil thus death prey on us so.</u>

So I say unto you, live by your moral values and do not invite people who are not morally correct and clean; of your moral values and cleanliness in your life, land and or country; environment. This is your right as citizens of your land. Why let someone that has no moral values come into your land and erode the infrastructures you've build to safeguard you?

If a man was raised in a land that bask in war and religious lies, do not invite any in your land because they will not keep the peace in your land. Guaranteed they are going to take their dirty and unclean ways with them and they are going to stir up trouble in your land.

If a country and their people sell immorality in music, videos, movies, clothing, books and so forth, do not entertain these immoral things in your land. Guaranteed these immoral things are going to take away from the cleanliness of your land. Your values are not their values; so entertain nothing that is valueless and immoral. Immorality sink lands and bring about more immorality. Thus I plea with Lovey to separate good from evil because no one that is good can be clean in unclean lands and homes; societies.

Michelle

In all that I know and write, I know truth.

I know the value of life.
I also know death.

I know the evil dead can make you feel that they are still alive and well living with you in the living.

I know the cunningness of death; thus death play with the lives of the living.

Yes I know you cannot comprehend this because this knowledge you know nothing of.

When you have eyes you see.

When you have not; you are blind. Not as the blind man because the blind man's sight, is truly different from yours and mine.

Yes I know death and I know life, but in knowing life and death, death seek to kill you and do all to kill you.

We cannot live in true peace with death because in truth, the average man knows neither life nor death. Both roads are painful. One more painful than the other, thus we were given a choice.

Some will win.
Some will fail.

Some will have a saving grace; lifeline.
Some truly do not.

Some will live
And
Billions will die.

Michelle
January 09, 2016

It's weird
It's odd
The way life is

Confusing, therefore, I have many questions.

Yes my journey continues and as I travel solo, I am being warned about the men in Cuba.

I am shown them painted in gold like masqueraders going to carnival. Thus I am being warned to stay away from Cuban Men. All that glitters is truly not gold, but painted on to fool the unsuspecting visitor.

I see the women working, Cuban women working hard. They are the labour force and they do work hard. They are dressed in blue and they do get bit by dogs; meaning they do work hard as slaves for little pay.

So as I journey to Varadero, Cuba solo, I truly do not know what to expect. Therefore, I am hoping and praying Lovey journey with me and make everything alright with me and him. The warning signs are there and I truly have to make Lovey the head and all of me.

I cannot stray from him and I truly hope he does not make a shirt or a skirt make me stray from him. He is my cause and need despite us not being on the same page.

So yes, I am hoping that he journey's with me despite me failing him in his book.

I am hoping, and it is my good and true will for 2016 and beyond that he Lovey comes truly clean with me so that all we do from beginning to end can and will be truly clean.

It's a new year and new beginning; thus 2016 should be the year that we (Lovey and I) mend our broken fences and truly make them impenetrable to all the forces of evil everywhere. Not just on or in earth, but in the spiritual realm and where all evil resides.

Michelle
January 09, 2016

As 2016 has begun, it is my hope and good will that the rest of the year brings me true joy and happiness.

It is my hope and true good will that I find true peace and goodness in all that I do for others including me.

In all the true giving I do unto others, I hope and pray that my goodness of truth bring those I give; goodness, good and true prosperity, true blessings, true peace, true honesty, cleanliness, true wealth, good and positive health, life, thoughts of goodness and truth so that they can build themselves positively in a good and true way and intern help others positively in a good and true way.

It is my hope that I can travel to good lands in Africa and beyond in 2016; if not, 2017 and beyond.

As for my heavy and burdened spirit, it is my good and true hope including will that 2016 is the year that my financial and spiritual burdens more than disappear in a good and positive way more than infinitely and indefinitely forever ever without end.

It is my good and true will that I am released from my spiritual shackles and chains.

My good and true will that the heaviness that is on me and around me be lifted more than indefinitely from on and around me.

MY GOOD AND TRUE WILL FOR 2016 AND BEYOND

It is my good and true will that I am released from the spiritual prison that has held me captive here on earth so that I cannot rise and do my good and true works for humanity.

It is my good and true will for 2016 and beyond that all the evils and evil spirits that surround me and do me harm be jailed; housed and locked in hell more than forever ever without end so that they cannot hurt me ever again and or anymore.

It is my good and true will for 2016 and beyond that all the goodness I've received in the spiritual realm be added unto me in a good, clean, positive and true way here on earth so that I can do more good works for all the good and true people of this earth that is in need.

This good and true blessing must also help earth; the environment of earth and the universe including the true and living God; Lovey and my gorgeous and beautiful mother, Rosalind Rosetta Morgan.

Michelle

As 2016 move forward and the days turn into nights and the nights turn into days, it is my good and true will that he Lovey find what he is truly looking for.

It is my hope, good and true will for 2016 and beyond that the spiritual wicked and physically wicked (males and females), stop taking and or stop robbing me of my financial wealth, strength and prosperity; including my physical and spiritual health.

As 2016 has begun, I hope and pray as it is my good and true will that my children will do better for themselves and start achieving in a positive and clean way.

It is my good and true will that they might find truth in me and Lovey as well as in the good that they do for others and self.

It is my good and true will for 2016 and beyond for them; that they find their good and true ambition and cleanliness and work towards it.

It is my good and true will for 2016 and beyond that they break ties from negative influences and do what is truly good, right and best for them, the environment, Lovey and Me including the good others that they will meet in their lives.

It is my good and true will for self and Lovey that 2016 and beyond see black people; our good and true people break away from all evil and negative influences positively and start walking good, true, clean and honest to him Lovey in a good and true way.

It is my hope, good and true will that; black people truly find their way and begin to live right.

It is my hope, my good and true will for 2016 and beyond; that black people truly break away from death by relinquishing all their Babylonian ties including language, praise and worship including clothing.

It is my good and true will for self and Lovey and our good and true people that we walk upright in truth and righteousness, morally, ethically, spiritually and physically to him always without straying.

It is my good and true will here in 2016 and beyond that the physical and spiritual evil stop hindering us and stop causing us to stray.

It is my good and true will for 2016 and beyond that humans think of the earth and environment they live in and do all they can to save it so that they can truly live beyond tomorrow.

It is my good and true will here in 2016 and beyond, that all who are walking on the pathway of Lovey, to walk freely and never be hindered by the physical and spiritual wicked every again. Lovey we need this right away. You cannot linger anymore on your protection of us come on now.

It is my hope and good will that they (the good and true) find true peace and hope in all that they do for life and in life; Lovey.

It is my good and true will for self and Lovey and our good and true people that we think of earth and do all that is positive to clean her (Earth) up so that we can sustain and maintain her in a good and true way.

We can no longer destroy earth because in truth, we are destroying our mother and the land of our birth.

It is my good and true will for self, Lovey and our good and true people; that the Cayman Islands leave the coral reef and Caribbean Sea intact. No new shipping docks or piers or wharfs must be built to destroy the beauty of the sea more than indefinitely. The financial greed of man; humans do not outweigh the beauty of life. It is not humans alone that have life. The waters of this earth and or planet are our life force and saving grace; when we destroy it, we destroy self. Thus having nothing left. <u>Greed must never take precedence over life and this humanity truly needs to learn. When we take all from life now, what about tomorrow?</u>

What tomorrow do your children and grandchildren; future generations have?

We must preserve because tomorrow comes for others, not just you.

You Lovey want and need your home in the Cayman Islands; thus Cayman Islands must be preserved and left clean and whole. The people of Cayman must preserve you come on now.

Cayman can no longer accommodate greed and whoredom.

You Lovey asked me to do something for you and I give you my word, that I will not build or buy you your good and true home in a land that values not environmental life. If Cayman destroy my true love of the seas; waters, then Cayman must be destroyed because they preserve not truth; true life, the home you wanted your home in.

You saw it befitting to want and need a home there; thus greed and all facets of evil must be taken from that land forever ever without end. All evil must flee; thus Cayman is not the Devil's Island or cay. Evil and death must no longer walk on that land because this is the land you've chosen for your home Lovey, and they the people of Cayman must preserve you and your home more than indefinitely forevermore without end.

Remember you did not choose Jamaica. You said Jamaica is unclean and I know why. The murder rate, gun violence, scamming, human and animal sacrifices, murders, rape, pedophilia, prostitution, whoredom, religious lies and so much more that happens on the island daily caused Jamaican and Jamaica to lose their crown and place with you indefinitely.

Yes I still hold my true Jamaica dear to my heart because the Jamaica I build and give you, is true to my good and clean; pure and true heart of thee that is violence and sin free; void of all sin and evil as well as negative energy.

Michelle
January 2016

I am going to interrupt the flow of this book. It's January 11, 2016 and my dream world continues to be extremely different. I am not seeing death and destruction for a change, but it is different trust me on that.

I guess it's because I am going away solo and I am scared. I am going to a place and or country that I truly do not know nor do I know anyone.

There are restrictions such as language. I am truly restricted in Spanish thus the language barrier that I will face. Culture wise, I am not afraid because I am an island girl.

The food will be different as to taste but we will truly see. Like I said it's January 11 and this afternoon I had this really weird dream. In the dream I went to this dentist. He was dressed in full white and he was tall and lanky; weird looking. The picture that came to mind in the dream is that Merchant gentleman. You know the one that likes to dance and lip sync. I don't know if I've spelt his name right but you have the picture of the dentist I am talking about. Please note, in the dream it is implied that it is this Merchant fellow, **but implied does not mean it's the person.** *You are just given a feature as to what to look for I guess; if that's the correct explanation. The gentleman and or dentist in the dream had the same height but was a bit skinner than the implied Merchant. Shave off half off say about 20 to 30 pounds Merchant's weight and you get the image of how tiny this dentist is in weight.* **AND YES HE WAS BRITISH AND OR HAD THE BRITISH ACCENT.**

In the dream after he had performed his duties on my mouth he went by this sink to turn on the water for me to wash my mouth out. The outer layer was red and the inside white. The sink is a rectangular shape and for illustration purposes only, I am going go to Google to see if I can find the exact image of the sink I am talking about and or something similar.

I went over to where he was and he said bend over. Mind you I had whitey silver clothing and or a top on. He lifted up my clothing and I did not have any underwear on and he tried to put his ding dong in my Naa Na. Mind you, he could not get it in because my legs were closed. I wasn't into sex with him I wanted something different. But in the dream he was a sex man that did not like to touch your breasts or have oral sex.

He did not like kissing either but somehow we kissed and it was then, he disclosed to me the pill he was taking for AIDS and I said to myself in the dream; I've contacted AIDS because you can get AIDS through saliva. He was trying to tell me I could not get it (AIDS) due to the pill he was taking.

I said to him when does he want me to come back and he said in two weeks. I wanted to make an appointment with his secretary and he told me his secretary doesn't work all the time. She was away or something like that. She was away on a coffee run because when she came back she asked who left two dollars on her desk. Please note, I did not see her, I just heard her. Yes this dream scares me in the living because in the dream these sexual acts occurred in his office and not elsewhere. So I am gathering in the living and not in my dream world that someone of English and or British lineage is having sexual intercourse with unsuspecting ladies unprotected and knowingly spreading HIV/AIDS.

So females whether Black, White or Asian and yes Indian, please check yourself for AIDS and or HIV if you are having unprotected sex with your White Male English Doctor. And no, I am not singling out England and or Britain. This doctor could be in New Zealand, Australia, Tanzania, South Africa, or he could be one of those doctors that go to remote countries in Africa or Europe giving special aide.

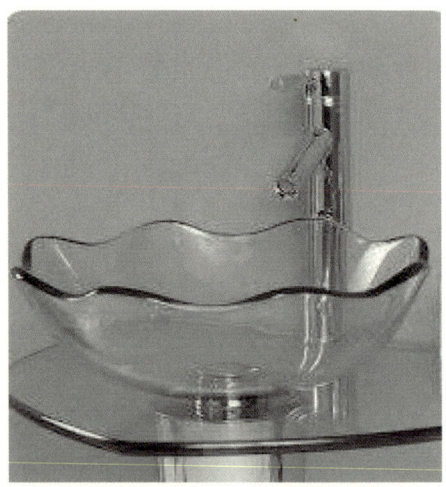

This picture is not even close to the image of the sink in the dentist office. The sink was more rectangular and it was not glass but porcelain, if porcelain is what they make bathroom sinks out of. The reason why I chose this image is because of the curves. The sink in his office had curves but not much. Oh man I so can't explain the sink correctly. But trust me the sink was gorgeous; of class, so this dentist is truly not poor. And if I've confused you in the description of the sink, I am truly sorry because this is the best I can do. I so can't draw either because if I could, I would draw the picture for you.

And I am so sorry that I could not give you a description of his secretary but like I said, I did not see her, I only heard her.

I am sorry I could not give you a better description of this guy but keep the image of Merchant especially the nose. Glasses he did not wear but truly don't quote me on the glasses. Keep the nose for sure. Maybe you can put this puzzle together because I can't. If the picture do not apply, use the red rectangular and curved porcelain sink as your reference.

Michelle

So as I journey real soon to a land that is not known to me Lovey, let us journey in true peace and happiness and not turmoil.

Let the land, people and sea find good favour in me and you. Oh Lovey, we have to bathe in the sea, so please let the waters of the sea be nice and warm and void of all impurities for me and you. Lovey, we have to truly enjoy the water of the sea come on now.

Let the land, people and sea bless us bountifully with truth, warmth, true love, clean clear and healing waters so that we can enjoy day after day for our say there. Let us meet truly loving people that are friendly, honest, helpful and kind, and not people that do to get.

As we travel together Lovey, let the sun and waters heal my aching and decaying body.

Let all impurities that is in me and on me be eradicated indefinitely from me and yes you too Lovey.

Let us bask in the organic fruits of the land Lovey.

Let us drink organic coffee and eat organic food that is good for us to eat and drink.

So as the land, sea and people receive us in goodness and in truth, receive them also in goodness and in truth and bless them continually.

Let the people start doing to rebuild their lives in a good, true, clean and positive way.

So as we journey good and true to Varadero, Cuba, let us come back to Canada; Toronto, Canada good and true without incident of the negative and sinful including positive kind.

So as I take your hand in truth Lovey, take mine also and let's journey free and true without incident, whoredom, theft, violence, death, illness, negative forces and incidents including negative elements. Let us truly relax and have a good time because this is our place; the place I chose for us to go have fun and to relax.

So as Bob Marley said, "I know a place where we can carry on," let's carry on Cuba in a good, clean, fun and true way.

Michelle

As I close this book in goodness and in truth, I just want to state that rebellion is truly not violence.

Rebellion is doing the little things that are positive in life to help you build yourself. Yes it's hard but you have to think of you.

Know that your dictator doesn't have to be and isn't your politician alone. **<u>Your dictator is also the clergy man or woman that leads you astray.</u>**

Your dictator is also your spouse and or partner that abuse you and control your life.

You dictator is also your children that abuse you and steal all from you.

No one should live in fear and in undesirable situations thus your financial institutions, your boss and the company you work for that is causing you pain is also your dictator.

As humans we truly do not think of the lives we are hurting, and that is why MANY CAN COME IN AND OFFER US THEIR GODS AND SAY THEY ARE BETTER, WHEN WE KNOW TO OURSELVES THAT NO GOD IS BETTER THAN LOVEY; LIFE, THE TRUE AND LIVING GOD.

Michelle

Oh man it's early morning and I have to reopen this book. I cannot close it. Man I feel like a part of the accounting cycle when you open and close your books.

Anyway, before I get into my dreams because some of them I truly can't remember; I have touch base on these ones. In the Niagara Falls dream, I did not mention the small patch of ice that you could see in the dirt. The dirt was dark brown to black and ugly looking; nasty. See how the water flows over the edge of the falls. The small patch of ice was over the falls where the Maid of the Mist would go up to.

I also dreamt towards the beginning of the month that I was with Ronald Thwaites in Jamaica, and my body was riddled with ringworm. Man it was bad and nasty, so I am not sure if the school children of Jamaica is going to come down with ringworm. I just have to watch and see.

Now to my dreams because yesterday I was saying my computer is littered with Gully Bop and I dreamt about him. He was in black and white clothing; not in the bad sense. His white shirt had black imprints and like I said, this isn't bad nor is it a bad dream.

So Gully Bop, I give you the CLOWN CERTIFICATE NOT AWARD for 2015 and 2016.

No, I am truly not going to side with you, nor will I side with your Gold Digger. Firstly, you knew what was happening because you were not taken out of the loop. You knew the consequences of this because Nuffy or whatever his name is, was on Nightly Fix (hey Naro and yes I still can't see my book on your shelf) speaking about your involvement with Sting and how Shauna Chin was selected for you.

Everything that has happened to you, you called it upon yourself. You were a game and you are still a game. Laing saw an opportunity in you to cash in on your instant success and or clowning moments and he used it to his advantage and won.

The fact that you are with Shauna Chin says absolutely nothing for your character. You got what you deserved because you played the game, got used and lost. Now your dirty laundry is airing out on social media and you are a part of it.

You are using your life to stay relevant when in truth you are truly not. There is absolutely nothing desirable about you and Shauna Chin. Neither one of you represent the content and character of decent and civilized Jamaicans.

<u>Like I said, you are a clown; thus you are being clowned.</u>

You're a joke that was never truly relevant and you are going to stay a joke because in truth, I wouldn't download or buy your music. You came out of the depths of hell because a gully yu come from and wi all noa di gully dem inna Jamaica. You got a chance out of hell and instead of cleaning yourself up and making something better of yourself; you are still acting like the fool; the court gesture and clown for all of humanity to see and laugh at.

You've not brought dignity and respect to yourself nor have you brought it to dancehall. You've kept the gully dutty ways, thus no one will truly respect you.

You do for fame and to keep relevant, but someone that is not truly relevant in the beginning, cannot be truly relevant in the end.

Yu did dutty from mauning soh yu cannot come clean a evening, so truly stop because you are truly not innocent in any of this. You are as guilty as Laing and your associates.

An memba sey, ole people sey when yu a dig grave dig two.

Remember what you and Ninja Man did to Merciless.

WELL CONSIDER YOUR ASS WHOOPING BY SHAUNA CHIN VINDICATION FOR WHAT YOU DID TO MERCILESS.

You disrespected Merciless. You and Merciless have no beef. Ninja Man and Merciless have beef from Sting days of old, and you should have never interfered in something that did not concern you. You had no right to do this.

Yu wrang in many ways to have gotten involved. Thus you are being used. Ninja Man nuh fava yu, im jus play yu; thus you got your ass whooping fair and square. No I am not condoning what your gold digger did to you, but fair is fair; an ole people did sey, when yu a dig ole fi di nex man, dig two. One fi dem an one fi yu.

Know that Ninja Man is a part of Sting and he helped to build Sting, so im naugh lef Laing. All when yu hear Ninja Man a talk, he's still on the payroll of Laing. Laing a im daddy. No, truly don't go there bout Ninja bash Sting. Ninja Man a double wedged sword an im mouth mek fi talk crap sometimes.

Ninja cannot leave offa Laing name. The bashing wey yu si im Ninja a du; no matter the negativity that comes out of his mouth, he Ninja is promoting Sting. Ninja Man promote Sting and will forever promote Laing and Sting. All Ninja a talk, it's all publicity because im caane truly bash di han wey a feed him. Ninja Man a actor thus he acts in movies.

So truly take note Gully Bop and truly fade away. Reinvent yourself and truly stop letting people look down on Jamaicans because true and decent Jamaicans truly do not act like you. You are a clown and will always be a clown. Thus I've delivered my message and your message Lovey. It's time for people to grow up and act their age. Come on now. It's time for the self praise by ugly people to stop Lovey come on now. No, fi real Lovey, coo pan some a dem sinting dey wey sey dem a hat gyal an not even di demons of hell want dem. Dem so friggen ugly dat mirror run from dem. No Lovey, dem caane buy mirror because mirror run from dem. Wen mirra si dem a cum, mirror run an hide to regile.

Mirror nuh lie and mirror can't stan ugly; thus mirror run from dem. Bunch of self hating nastiness that truly do not represent the black community.

Coo pan dem to, bleach out, haggard out, tattooed out, fake haired out and more than ugly. No Lovey, some of these Hollywood execs should not hire makeup artists to put ugly on some of their actors; they should just go to some of these black communities and rent dem fi a dollar. The is plenty of ugly there. Truss mi Hollywood would save hundreds of millions of dollars on ugly because dem literally have ugly walking around in the living.

Thus it is my good and true hope that these self hating things that say they are black women and men, truly come to see the ugliness of self; them, and stop misrepresenting the black community and letting other nations look down upon us in a negative light.

We paint negative pictures of ugliness of self and when the global community lash out against us and say we are ugly, we have no one to blame but self. We as a race walk around with too much self hate; low self esteem, lack of morals and decency (dancehall it things), lack of truth and culture; no true identity and more.

So yes, in 2016 I am calling out the ugly people of the black community and putting them in a community all to themselves. In truth, they are truly not a part of the black race due to self hate and true ugliness come on now.

As for you Wally British, I did truly like you but after seeing your post, YU A SCAMMA. You are a grown as woman that I thought had principle, but from seeing your take on Shauna Chin and Gully Bop; you are a scammer and I truly hope people don't listen to you.

Whoredom is wrong period. It is truly disrespectful for men and women to cheat on each other. Both parties are showing each other that they do not have respect for each other. If you are with someone why cheat on them?

And no, I am not painting a perfect picture of myself because I've been there and done that in my younger days. The difference is, I've found truth and the truth of myself thus whoredom I truly stay away from. **It is a sin and it (cheating and or whoredom) does devalue you.**

As women, some of us have and has outlined the package that we want and need and stray from that package. We do not take the time to wait on that package to come along. Wi inna rush an pick up what is not on the list and or our package. Thus we cheat and this is wrong. Never deviate from the right course you are on for anything or anyone. In regards to Shauna Chin taking a man into Gully Bops house, she was wrong. An Gully Bop you should have known sey when yu tek up Delilah yu a go en up like

Samson and lose it all. Yu lucky. Thus walk good because di padlock was to kill yu, jus like Delilah killed Samson in her own devious way.

Yu artical because mi noh which man inna dem right head would pick up a Delilah and clown demself by saying they love har. But dem did sey love is blind and it truly is so far as I can see with you. Yu ha a good heart but truly do better and secure you.

Remember, you danced with the devil and the devil used you. Now what are you truly going to do?

So Wally British you are off my list once and for all because you are a scammer. You too are a Delilah because money is your ultimate goal. Thus Delilah's are not just females they are males also.

Dreamt I was in this restaurant; massive restaurant. Eva had put on a function and I was invited along with my sister. I saw Avalon there. Avalon is someone I went to high school with back in the day. It's so weird that I am dreaming about old class mates more and more. But never the less, Avalon was there. The table that we had there was fish cooking on this long steel table. There was a variety of fish like snapper and cod fish that was flat out. I call it cod fish because it was flat and looked nice. And yes I wanted that fish. I kept turning the fishes on the table for them to cook because I did not like the way they did not have colour in them. They looked steamed and not fried. An yu noa wi Jamaicans, wi affi ha colour inna wi meat and or salting. I don't know what happened but I think some of the people wanted to leave and or got up and left and Eva said you're not leaving; she spent too much money for the dinner. Suffice it to say they stayed. But some of the fish on the table got burnt; a little too done. We ate and then my sister got up to get this thing. I can't remember the name of it, but it was shinny and red; not red red as in the colour red but a fruity shinny red that was a bit smaller than grapes. I wanted to get some too but all I saw was grapes, globe grapes lots of them; so I didn't end up getting the fruity shinny red things my sister got.

People in the dream I wanted more food and I headed back to the table where the food was, but ended up bumping into this young Asian guy. He was in a blue suit and on the right part of the suit at the chest area, he had some white flakes on it. He liked Eva but was afraid to tell her. Man was he ever shy. I asked him if he wanted me to introduce him to her and he said no, he was scared. He was so in love with her that I think he did not want to act the fool around her due to his shyness. Any hoo, he ended up giving me some pineapples on my plate. I also had this spatula in my hand that had a piece of food hanging from it. Going back to the table all I saw was waitresses; white waitresses cleaning up. They had turned some of the massive dining hall and or restaurant into a parking lot setting where cars could park. I thought that weird, thus I did not get any food. I somehow ended up at this gift shop where my sister was buying gifts. She bought a gift that cost over fifty dollars. To me the gifts were not worth it because they were small. One particular gift I saw was for $3.88 but I did not buy it because they were not to my liking nor were they worth it. The gifts had perfume in them but they were children's gifts not adult gifts.

My sister and I ended up separating again but this time the building and or place that we were in shock and fell apart. The place was crumbling and people were falling. You couldn't really get out. I went to this area and I saw the WWE President Vince McMahon walking with these two gentleman and they were singing. They went to use the elevator but could not use the elevator because the cable wires had snapped and you could see this from the destruction that was in the elevator. So here I am going to watch and see in the living if someone dies in the WWE again.

Somehow I managed to get outside and was on a winding car port driveway and you could see people jumping to get to safety.

Like I said, I truly do not want to decipher dreams in 2016. I truly don't know my true family and people. Maybe there is going to be another earthquake in Japan that destroys the country. But I truly do not know why my mind has Shanghai China on it. So maybe somewhere in Asian land destruction cometh.

This dream is confusing for me because I did see Avalon and I did see Vince McMahon. So yes death is masking death and I just have to watch and see which land is devastated. And yes the white man in 2015 did tell me Japan and Jamaica is going to be destroyed. So yes I have to wait and see because like I've told you, males in the spiritual realm do lie; tell you lies. If it was a female, black female that told me these lands were going to be destroyed, I would hold her word to be true and correct, but men I am truly leery of and I stay away from.

Males in the spiritual realm when it comes to their words hold no value to me. Trust me you know the liars in this realm as well as the physical realm; thus he Lovey has to deal with the lies of men that they put in their so called holy book of lies and deceit, whoredom, incest, war and violence. This book they call the holy bible, but no book can be holy if it teaches you to tell lies and spread lies; hate.

Michelle